Prison Segmentation For Spousal Support

Rev. Mike Wanner

Table Of Contents

Introduction

America alone has more than 2.3 million people in jail or prison.

I like most people was entirely oblivious to that fact. I started channeling Angel Raphael in 2013 and began releasing little message sets as they came through.

In message set 16 of the Angel Raphael Speaks Series there was an invitation for me. Here is that message:

"I asked Mike to Step into Prison Energetically

I have asked Mike to get the address and location within a prison of a designated space so he can visit energetically and receive feedback for us. Whether he will have time, interest or opportunity to do this will be interesting to see. As he writes this, he is not thrilled with the idea. We are already consuming a lot of his time."   ARS16

1 - What is Prison Segmentation

The main idea of Prison Segmentation is to use what is available in new ways that can improve the quality of the incarceration experience for prisoners, prison staff, taxpayers, and the families of them all. New ideas and creativity for what can be done at no additional cost are to be encouraged.

Facilities can endeavor to create a B shift and a C Shift that will offer great new freedom possibilities for prisoners. Being able to select patterns or tracks of segmentation that carries opportunities will promote feelings of personal empowerment and peace.

The lessening of feelings of overcrowding within the facility may reduce risks for staff and prisoners alike.

Many stories share some unplanned segmentation of groups of inmates where they have grouped themselves based on ethnic or cultural orientations or other common interest. The concept shared here is not organized to work against those choices of alignment by prisoner's interests but to increase freedom and space.

This concept should prove helpful to all prisoners and staff by spreading out the residents and allowing more space per prisoner at many times.

Each facility that chooses to make some adjustments based on this idea could receive security benefits by having residents spread throughout the building around the clock.

Furthermore, this idea could have stress reduction throughout, and prisoners who are at higher risk may be more readily separated from potential conflicts with others.

So Far, I have drafted a number of ideas about segmentation and published them:

Prison Segmentation For Safety, And Sanity, Security, Peace, and Space
Prison Segmentation For Security
Prison Segmentation For Mental Peace
Prison Segmentation For Joint Ventures
Prison Segmentation For Startup Ideas
Prison Segmentation For Your Rehabilitation: R U Ready?
Prison Segmentation For Family Villages
Prison Segmentation For Senior Prisoners
Prison Segmentation For Coaching Clubs
Prison Segmentation For Miracles

There is much more that can be developed. You can play a big part in creating all that is needed to help you and many others.

2 - Dedication

This writing is dedicated to the spouses of prisoners who are trying as best they can to understand the situation that has landed on them and their spouses and all the other extended family members who have been impacted by the incarceration.

There is so much about the legal system that is counter-intuitive and difficult to comprehend. As I continue to develop material, the complexity of incarceration facilities and processes continue to amaze me.

Not every prisoner is fortunate enough to have a spouse who can help them so the ones who do would be wise to appreciate the efforts begun on their behalf. Some prisoners without spouses may have other family members who can help, and they also should be treasured and thanked.

Prison is not easy, and prisoners need to be aware that efforts to help them are tedious, time-consuming and draining on many levels. While results are desired and possible, projects can take a long time to accomplish and require a lot of effort.

Prisoners can find patience will serve them well. Advocates have a lot of steps to take, and an essential thing for prisoners to consider is that gratitude for each bit of effort can help your supporters to keep working for your benefit.

Resources for those with limited funds can be challenging to engage. Prisoners who are fortunate enough to have advocates could make sure they do not burn out by being continuously grateful.

It seems that confinement makes all efforts towards freedom very difficult. Success will only occur when persistence has followed decisiveness long enough to reach new plateaus of possibility.

The time you have left in your life can be spent in regret, resentment, anger, fear, hatred, and despair of you can choose to choose positive efforts that can upgrade your quality of life. Working toward a goal can bring a feeling of peace, harmony, hope, joy, and purpose.

Your creator has instilled you with free will about your life and your efforts. If your past actions have been ill-advised, you can change your thinking and your future endeavors, so your new results are better.

3 - Are You Grateful

If the answer is no, then you may be making a big mistake. It is easy to judge the efforts of others and get it wrong.

Effort does not always bring results to the prison community. The laws and institution of jurisprudence are very complicated and intricate processes are needed to reverse judgments that have been handed down.

Judgments of courts are not set up to be easily changed unless circumstances make it a priority issue. Many may think that fairness is lacking, but that does not change the law and the sentences that had been set.

Years ago in Philadelphia, there was a bank that had a saying "Wishing won't do it – Saving Will" and it was cute and meaningful. Regarding prison, you might consider creating your own saying or jingle.

Perhaps something like "Moaning is a waste of time – Creating new ideas can change my life." Or perhaps, " I can do better, and I Will."

Prisons are stressful because there a lot of people who want attention and an insufficient number of people who can initiate change.

Whether you are guilty or innocent makes little difference to the institution that houses you. The way you are treating the ones trying to help you can make a huge difference in how they are able to continue to motivate themselves.

In many situations, the person closest to someone who is caught up in it can feel the desperation more intensely than the one impacted. When there are little hope and little appreciation, motivation can die, and faith can be abandoned.

If you have someone who is championing you, please be wise and offer them your gratitude and return their love. When you start each new day, you can change your thinking patterns and your future.

4 - True Love Knows a Lot

True love is difficult to comprehend even when there is freedom for all and interaction when desired. Separate the parties and everything can become more difficult

Communication between prisoners and spouses can be little to nothing in the complex prison arrangement that exists in today's' incarceration facilities. Every threat that is made to the security of prisons can be responded to with new levels of separation and isolation.

The obstacles to love and communication make the rehabilitation process more difficult and success less likely. Physical obstructions are not mental obstacles.

The powers of the mind are impressive when applied in an optimal way. Unfortunately for many prisoners, it is challenging to understand those abilities when you have little or no feedback that allows an incremental valuation and feedback.

Your mind is so powerful that it can change many things if the belief is held long enough without the need for confirmation. If you know the truth in your heart, that fact can radiate out and stimulate a return flow of the same resonance as you sent.

The variable is time. The risk is that uncertainty leads easily to frustration and a resulting short-circuiting of the fundamental resonance.

I am hopeful that the concept that I share can be embraced and finessed to the degree that your thinking predicts your results.

5 - The Fragility of Each Person

The whole human connection in space and time is susceptible to the emotions of time and place and people and music and many things. Health and wellness have roots in how one feels, what one feels they can do, what they are motivated to do and the freedom to do what they choose.

The harmonics of alignment can influence that which is reverberating in that space and any new reverberations added to that area. In music, you can hear when an instrument is not vibrating in balance with others. Life is similar.

People can be in the balance or out of balance in many circumstances. When people have their balancers, it can be relatively easy for them to move along in life.

I am pretty happy with the way things are in my life, but when I started connecting with the energy of prisons, I was experiencing an uneasy state of mind. Even though I was invited by the Angels to make the connections, there was an ill at ease feeling of stress.

As soon as I would think about family, the stress would fade away quickly. Focus back to the prisons; pressure could return immediately.

Challenged was I, but not threatened. I knew the trigger, and I knew the antidote.

I could proceed quite nicely by Angel connecting or family thought whenever I needed to break an uneasy link.

Prisoners may not be as empowered as I am since they are not in control of their circumstances and/or may not be as aware of the mental tools that I use. Patterns of thinking can be beneficial for controlling feelings when a person knows that they can take charge.

More often than not, people may have a tendency to feel limited by circumstance and accept the reality they see. Prison would not be the first choice of a location to choose for inspiration.

In the outside world, family space can be a place of safety where creativity can flow without effort. Prison can give the opposite effect.

When someone comes to prison because they made some mistakes and are mandated into a new lifestyle that is more difficult than what they were familiar with, life can be downright hard. Without family in a place with a negative vibration, one will not be as able to feel safe and reclaim their powers or personal empowerment.

The daily cycles will not likely get easier until something positive happens but in prison that can take a long time. Other prisoners are not necessarily the most friendly and gregarious people on the planet.

Without the safety of family connectivity, depression and vulnerability may hit new levels of trouble for prisoners. Depression of prisoners can spread like a virus since there are many stories that indicate that mental illness is not unusual in prison.

6 - Your Fragility

Freedom is fantastic. Free People may make more mistakes than others, especially when they are young and dumb and operating with a mind that is still in development.

It is clear that society needs to take action to ensure that safety prevails throughout the land. Government is the agent of the people and those in office need to engage their responsibilities seriously while still being prudent.

Once the citizens are threatened by an individual, it is complicated for government agents as objective observers to justify their efforts to let anyone go free again. While there are processes like probation in existence that can release prisoners, recidivism indicates that failure of releases is very typical.

The decisions are very hard to make when safety is a prominent value. The jobs of the evaluators are not easy as their determinations leave them also subject to judgment.

Your job if you choose to accept it is to make the decision for them easier by stacking up the evidence in a way that indicates an affirmative ruling is the right one. This could take a lot of work, and you have to choose for yourself if you are willing to build all that.

Of course, you will say yes but are you really willing to do all that work. It is likely that a part of you will have a long involved argument that rattles around in your head saying something like "This is totally unfair."

You have the opportunity to choose what thoughts you listen to and which of them motivate you or paralyze you. You have power but also vulnerability.

Your creator has given you free will which is a double-sided sword which can hurt your challenges but also yourself. Diligent control of your thinking is the primary survival tool for prisoners.

Your decisions are changeable but also final in the minute they are thought and each thought impacts on the time it is being considered and the results of that interval of your life. Please be diligent in your decisiveness.

7 - Reconnecting Fractured Families

Citizens have a tendency to grow up in a family and if they get arrested and sent to jail then that peace of sanity is fractured by their conviction.

Prisoners who have their own spouse and children can leave behind many more entanglements than single folks. Those connections can be helpful on many levels or complicated depending on many factors.

Spousal support being the focus of this book brings me back to the topic and the importance of patience and gratitude on the part of the prisoners.

My books about segmentation can offer a buffer that could help prisoners to find the quiet and teamwork necessary to discuss, plan and initiate efforts that can show spouses that they are appreciated after all. At the same time, a community focus on appreciation can offer prisoners increased awareness of the kinds of things they can do to show appreciation to their spouses.

Prisoners working together who can focus on the spousal support without the interference of other prisoners can develop a whole new appreciation that can help all participants to process reality in a positive way that can increase understanding and planning.

8 - Spousal Visits

It seems that most prisons in America do not allow spousal visitation for prisoners. While this may make some sense for short-term detention, the longer stays can leave prisoners feeling very disconnected from their families.

There has been a lot written about prisoners paying the price for their crimes and not being rewarded when they are supposed to be paying their debt. In other places, you can find reference to babies being born as a result of spousal visits and the state should not be helping to produce children who will be raised by single parents and possibly need state support.

While those opinions are surfacing from citizens, there may be another level of conversation that is being lost. The prisoners have needs also and denying them is not helpful towards rehabilitation.

Being separated from family is hard for prisoners, and there is an additional hardship on the spouses who may have little resources to handle all that has been dumped on them.

Spousal support teams can focus on creating messages where possible to send to the spouses that empathize with the challenges and declare appreciation for the individual problems of each spouse. Men especially need to take time and identify specific challenges, so spouses know that you understand the depth of their struggle. Catch all phrases should be avoided.

Spelling it out will be music to the spousal ears as everybody wants to be understood.

9 - Getting Past Your Anger

The detail for your spouse is essential and here is why. In prison, it is likely that no one is willing to listen to you.

You can see that you would feel less than cooperative with those who did not listen to you. Prisoners may not feel pleasant about their situation and be friendly to those who live in the same space as they do.

Not feeling well about the people near you can hurt them and you. As you retain negative energy in your feeling towards your situation and domicile, that can be disharmonious to life, your fellow neighbors and yours.

Teamwork that can flow in segmentation can allow many holes in community association to be filled as you have a group rethink of possibilities to send love to the families of all.

A simple way to increase integration and peaceful interaction is to have each member of the team who talks about spousal support share about their families in as much detail as they are comfortable.

When you learn about others, your humanity can be triggered and peacefulness within can be a byproduct. I would encourage everybody to be upfront and open about inviting sharing as desired.

While not required, participants could suggest that they would like prayers for individuals or situations. Praying for others is a great way to find your personal peace.

10 - Childcare Considerations

A significant issue for prisoner spouses is to try to fund, balance, work, and parent with only one set of arms and a limited income.

I wrote a whole separate segmentation book about an idea for a family to live together in a Family Village. The dynamic of the village could potentially improve all the lives of all the participants.

The prisoner could parent and/or homeschool while the spouse earned a living that could support the whole process.

The prisoner parent could be motivated and feel they had a purpose in their life and be a part of the family team that was able to bring up the child or children in a much more regular manner than if the prisoner was away in prison and the spouse had the sole responsibility to parent the child.

Both parents would bear the entire responsibility for their child at the Village, and neither the prisons, any governmental overseers, any developers, managers or overseers would be responsible for occupant child care or supervision in any way.

I understand that you may think that I am just dreaming, but my primary purpose in writing is to accept that invitation from the Angel Of Healing - Raphael. Healing brings possibilities.

Accepting reality as permanent is not a good idea. Creative thought has excellent power when it is supported by Prayer and positivity.

11 - Spouses Struggle

The same unwanted change that impacts prisoners also affects the spouses and the children, and it can all be overwhelming with limited resources of support.

While there are some government programs to help somewhat, the isolation of a single parent is hard. Extended families can help, but not everybody has one which is in a position to help.

Churches and community organizations try in their own ways to do what they can, but the challenges are tremendous. There is no single thing that can be done that can replace the solidness of a loving family.

The parent struggling to keep on keeping on has an uphill battle and has to be a great balancer to optimize the results of efforts. One idea to help is not to rely too heavily on a single source of support.

Critical trauma patients are sometimes put on a rapid infuser so all that they need can be delivered quickly. How beautiful it would be for spouses of prisoners to receive a timely infusion of love and support from their spouse and also a team of prisoners with spouses who can add to the volume needed.

Further need filling could happen when prisoners invite their spousal support group partners to reach out and encourage their spouses to have similar support groups on the outside. Just the suggestion could help prisoner's spouses to find a community who they could reach that could take the edge off the loss of their spouse for a time so they can get a mental break.

Prisoners and their groups working inside and the spouses and their teams working to connect outside could efficiently bridge somewhat the community gap that prison perpetuates.

While the groups offer nowhere near the comfort that spouses provide each other, they would be much more understanding than the general populations outside or inside. Having a commonality of problems allows understanding.

Prayer partners can also flow from these alignments as hearts open to the struggles of others and the wanting to do something to help blooms. There can be a triggering dynamic of helping others to a much higher degree than one would do for themselves.

Losing yourself in the struggle of yourself can lead to fear, anxiety, and depression. Losing yourself in the issues of another allows you relaxation and perspective and purpose.

So, giving your attention to others can be great for the giver. Giving and receiving within a group can benefit everybody in the group.

Sharing within the group allows each participant to get a reality check where they can plan together realistically so that each participant is ready to not overwhelm their spouse with expectations that the spouse cannot afford.

12 - Priming the Pump of Flow

Inside and out we are talking about giving and receiving in a group that can benefit all participants. In the early days of America, water was drawn from the ground with a pump that was powered by hand where a long handle was pushed up and down to bring the water up the tube to the spigot through vacuum pressure generated by the pumping.

When there was an interruption in the vacuum in the pump, the water would not flow. The answer to the dilemma was to "Prime" the pump.

The pump was primed by getting water into the tube so that the vacuum could be reestablished. When the pump was primed and air circuit restored, the circulation could continue.

Prison is an interruption of circulation between the spouses. The connection needs to be reestablished, and that can be difficult to do because the bond is less vibrant in the memory of each spouse.

As separation continues so does that interruption of circulation. The traditional way for prisoners to re-enter the community outside the walls is a sudden shift back to freedom, but none of the support that a prisoner found before may be still available to them.

The comfort that a prisoner expects to find outside may be replaced by stark realities outside unless a ramp to success is built while still inside. Segmentation may be just the right tool.

Other segmentation groups have been suggested to work on preparing for reentry. There is a lot that can be done in segmentation that could never happen in general population.

Segmentation may have a very beneficial impact on reducing recidivism. Please check to see if there are other groups that could help you.

The Prison dynamics of segmentation form a new base for building a future for all prisoners, but there is need of a rally around the group to support. The team to rally around is the spouses who have so little to work with and are expected to do so much.

The impact of this project involves millions and millions of Americans. Estimates or Guesstimates for perspective:

- 2.3 Million Prisoners
- 2.7 Million Children of Prisoners
- 2.3 Million Mother's of Prisoners
- 2.3 Million Father's of Prisoners
- 2.0 Million Spouses of Prisoners
- 2.5 Million Siblings of Prisoners

14.1 Million People

13 - Relighting Community

Prison policies can impact prisoners and families in many ways, and one can be the feeling of separation in a crowd. In a prison community, there is a guardedness that prevents one from really relaxing and drawing support from those around you.

That guardedness may lead to a distancing pattern which could keep distancing going even after the guardedness is no longer needed. That trend could prevent reconnecting later when a prisoner sets out to enter the community outside the walls.

I invite all in segmentation to let down the wall when you know you are safe. The earlier you can endeavor to reestablish one connection at a time, the better you can get at it and the faster you can create others.

Try to leave your fears and anxieties in prison so not to pollute the environment when you get home. Arriving home as an emotionally stable individual will allow a smooth transition.

Your family and friends will need to adjust to you as much as you will them so being together yourself will make it easier for them and then you and all of you and them together.

Before you even get out, Segmentation can really smooth your time.

14 - Giving Is Healing

As you read this book, I am hopeful that you understand that you have new potentials available. You can change your life if you choose to change your mind.

I share thoughts that I love:

"A rich life is lived from a giving heart, not a selfish mind."
— Rasheed Ogunlaru

"God tells you where to look; love tells you what to see."
— Matshona Dhliwayo

"People who give the best are those who give of themselves – your time, talents, words, knowledge."
— Omoakhuana Anthonia

"What you do for others, God will do for you."
— Dragos Bratasanu

"If you don't receive enough, have a look if you give enough."
— Jennifer White - Strong Heart Awakening

"A giver's purse can never be paused."
— Michael Bassey Johnson, Master of Maxims

"Give without expectation and receive with reckless abandon."
— Colleen Mariotti, Livology: A Global Guide to a Deliberate Life

"We are treated exactly the way we expect to be treated by the world and its people."
— Alaric Hutchinson, Living Peace

"Something must go within to bring what is within out. Oh yes! You need something within to bring
what is within out!"
— Ernest Agyemang Yeboah

"Never underestimate the power of giving a book!"
— Carmela Dutra

"Just like you can't reap a harvest without planting seeds, so you can't get without giving."
— Debasish Mridha

"The Dark Powers have to give before they can take."
— Stephen King, The Plant

"Selflessness. It should be the basis of every relationship. If a person truly cares about you, they'll get more pleasure
 from the way they make you feel, rather than the way you make them feel."
— Colleen Hoover, Confess

"And now you ask in your heart, 'How shall we distinguish that which is good in pleasure from that which is not good?'
Go to your fields and your gardens, and you shall learn that it is the pleasure of the bee to gather honey of the flower.

But it is also the pleasure of the flower to yield its honey to the bee.

For to the bee, a flower is a fountain of life,
And to the flower, a bee is a messenger of love,
And to both, bee and flower, the giving and the receiving of pleasure is a need and an ecstasy."
---Kahlil Gibran

"If you want to ask one question, ask yourself, what are you giving to the universe and only that will be returned."
— Amit Ray

"Some think that God rains money from heaven. These people can never be blessed because they themselves
have shut their door towards prosperity by not giving and telling others not to give."
— Paul Silway, Heaven I - Paradise: The City and Throne

"Love is bliss only if you are a giver, not otherwise."
— Tapan Ghosh, Faceless The Only Way Out

"Each of us will be remembered, either by those close to us or by those who have benefited from the greater good
which we have done."
— Donald Pillai

"Life is a balance between giving and receiving. The more you give, the more abundance will fill your life with joy."
— Debasish Mridha

"The best way to have in abundance is to give in essence. There is great possession in charity."
— Adewale Osunsakin, Time To Awake Christian Magazine

"The only way to heal is to help others heal, and the only way to find love and keep love in our lives is to give it to others."
— Dragos Bratasanu

"When I harvest my life right up to the edges, I have collected every last kernel of blessing."
— Erin M. Straza, Comfort Detox: Finding Freedom from Habits That Bind You

"Humans are givers by nature; that's why it's easier to do something for another than for oneself. Try it; you'll see what I mean."
— Charbel Tadros

"We often live as if our happiness depended on having. But I don't know anyone who is really happy because of what he or she has. True joy, happiness, and inner peace come from the giving of ourselves to others. A happy life is a life for others. That truth, however, is usually discovered when we are confronted with our brokenness."
— Henri J.M. N, Life of the Beloved: Spiritual Living in a Secular World

For
Considering
These
Ideas

Ever

It Does Not Help Prayer Still Does!

Resource: http://www.Create-A-Prayer.com

17 - Resource Books

Distant Healing Sessions (or Join Mail List) – Write To mikewann@voicenet.com

Books by Rev. Mike at www.Amazon.com

Veterans Healing Six Pack
1. *Trauma Healing Options for VA Hospitals: Help for Veterans to Own Their Healing and their future.*
2. *Trauma Healing Action Steps for Veterans: Help to Start Healing*
3. *Trauma Healing Action Steps for Veterans: Empowerment*
4. *Trauma Healing Action Steps for Veterans: Forgiveness*
5. *Trauma Healing Action Steps for Veterans: Thought Freedom*
6. *Tea For Veterans: Welcome One Home*

PTSD Power Pack:
1. *The PTSD Project: Turn Pain To Power*
2. *PTSD & Soul Retrieval: Putting One Back Together*
3. *PTSD & The Purple PAD: Calling all Scientists and PTSD Patients*

Angel Raphael Speaks Volume 1: Take Courage! God Has Healing in Store for You!
Angel Raphael Speaks Volume 2: Take Courage! God Has Healing in Store for You!
Angel Raphael Speaks Volume 3: Take Courage! God Has Healing in Store for You!
Angel Raphael Speaks Volume 4: Angels, Addicts, Alcoholics & Prisoners – Oh Yeah!
Angel Raphael Speaks Volume 5: Prisoners Caring for Alcoholics - Australia In Miniature Projects Intro
Angel Raphael Speaks Volume 6: Prisoners Caring for Addicts - Australia In Miniature For Addicts
Reiki Journaling from Japan
Reiki Is Alive: God's Great Gift
Four Parts /to Healing
Distant Healing: We Are All Connected
Stress Release Energy Work: How To Cope
Does Reiki Love Heal Cancer?
Group Consciousness
Salute To Philadelphia VA Medical Center: Thank You
Reiki Transcript for Reiki 2 & 3 Channels: Dr. Usui Is That You?
God Bless Kindle & Amazon
Puppies Are Different From People
If Your Dog Dies
Toy Guns Are Obsolete
Great Spirit Made Children With Red Skin: AND
The Cage of Fear: Is Not Locked
God Made Children Red, Yellow, Brown, Black & White: Greet Each Child...

Emergency Medical Kindness In The Cradle Of Liberty: Big City - Cracked Bell
Angels Are Always Around Addicts and Addicts: Help Is Near Now! Invite It In!
Angels Are Always Around Addicts and Alcoholics: Volume 2 - Tools To Help Re-Light...
Prison Jobs Now: Providing Care For Addicts And Addicts
Controlled Care Communities Concept
Prison Possibilities Dialogue Series: Concept
Prison Possibilities Dialogue Series: Volume 2, 3, 4, 5 Dialogues
Prison Possibilities Voluntary Exile
Prison Possibilities Corrections Coaches
Prison Possibilities For Mexicans: Is A Boat Better Than A Wall?
Prison Possibilities Family Time: A Reason to Thrive!
Prison Genius Pool: "So Much Genius In Jail."
Prison Possibilities Access Control: Prisoner Access by Request
Prisoner's Lawyers Can Save The American Economy: Make A Buck Doing It & ...
Prisoner Family Talks, Days, Stays & Vacations: Connecting Helps Healing
Prisoner Writing Projects: Write To Heal, Start Over & Reconnect
Prison Cell Clearing & Blessing: Clear Entities, Chase Ghosts, & Create Sacred Space
Prisoner Professors: Show You Are Aware Create Change With Care
Prison Reiki? Maybe Someday? A Gateway To Help Heal Prisons & America?
Judges and An Angel Rule On Possibilities: We Can Cut Sentences & Prison Costs
Ideas For Prison Wardens: Leadership Is Not Easy
Solitary Community: Could Community Support Cut Costs and Issues?
Prison Project Communications Team: Communications Can Change Lives
Motivating & Empowering Prisoners? Invite Prisoners To Find Their Motivation
Prison Segmentation For Safety, And Sanity, Security, Peace, and Space
Prison Segmentation For Security
Dowsing for Prisoners; Answers from Above
Ex-Prisoner Possibilities With Real Estate Investors
Prison Segmentation For Joint Ventures
Prison Segmentation For Your Rehabilitation: R U Ready?
Prison Segmentation For Family Villages
Prison Segmentation For Senior Prisoners
Prison Segmentation For Coaching Clubs
Prison Segmentation For Miracles

Little Books on Kindle.com by Rev. Mike:

English Medical History Questionnaire For Non-English Speakers
English Language Helper For Non-English Speakers
Wise Wonderful Women Are The Well Of The Family
Answers for Tests & Research: Dowsing Power
Crisis? Reiki! Baby? Reiki!
Bible References For Healing
Angel Raphael Speaks – Prisons
Angel Raphael Speaks – Veterans
The Saint Off Interstate 95

18 - Angels Please Prayers

Addict's

Angels of Healing Selected
Help Me to Stay Directed
Come To Me From The Sky
I Am Ready to Succeed Not Try
If I Don't Invite You In
I Might Not Win
I Have Been Lost For Too Long
Help Me To Stay Strong

Alcoholic's

Angels of Healing On High
Help Me to Stay Dry
Come To Me From The Sky
I Am Ready to Succeed Not Try
If I Don't Invite You In
I Might Not Win
I Have Been Lost For Too Long
Help Me To Stay Strong

From

http://AngelRaphaelSpeaks.com/AAAAAAA/

19 - Private Channeling

Angel Raphael Speaks a series of free messages that are channeled through Reverend Mike Wanner for the Highest good and Highest Healing of all concerned.

Many questions arise about Reverend Mike doing private channeling, and he does help with that so e-mail him.

Reverend Mike is available worldwide as a psychic channel, emotional release facilitator, spiritual energy practitioner & teacher, and public speaker. He looks forward to meeting you soon!

Email - mikewann@voicenet.com 215-342-1270 PRIVATE SPIRITUAL READINGS/channelings or Spiritual Healing Sessions: Telephone or in person. Rev. Mike is available for private, one-on-one intuitive sessions with you, his Guide Family, and your Guides. He helps by offering clarity on emotional situations about your life, your purpose, your spirituality, and the release of stuffed emotions and cellular memory.

Connect to the love of your Guides today!

Contact Rev. Mike for an appointment.

Sessions available:

Spiritual Readings
Angel Channeling
Distant Reiki Healing
Remote Clearing of Stuffed Emotions
Distant Clearing Cellular Memory
Distant Clearing Energy Blockages
Remote Clearing of the Chakras
Customized needs
Mastermind dowsing responses to yes/no direction finding
questions.

Rev. Mike is a facilitator of healing. He brings you and the Divine together so that you can align with the Divine and have a great time and a great life. All healing is between you and God, as it should be. Go ahead and start without Rev. Mike. Visit his prayer site http://www.Create-A-Prayer.com. Take the first step NOW.

20 - Reverend Mike Wanner

Rev. Mike Wanner started his Metaphysical and Ministerial studies with Reiki in 1993 and had studied seven styles of Reiki in the U.S., Japan, Canada, Denmark and Australia. He is certified to teach. He became certified to teach Integrated Energy Therapy in 1999 and co-taught the first IET class of the new Millennium. Mike began dowsing in 2001.

Ordained as a Metaphysical Minister of the International Metaphysical Ministry and an Interfaith Minister of the Circle of Miracles Ministry, Rev. Mike practices and teaches spiritual energy therapies in the Philadelphia Area.

Rev. Mike holds ministerial degrees from the University of Metaphysics and the University of Sedona. He is a Pastoral Care Associate at Aria - Frankford Hospital. He taught at the National Academy of Massage Therapy and Health Sciences.

Rev. Mike was a faculty member of the Medical Mission Sister's Center for Human Integration's School of Integrated Body/Mind Therapies in Fox Chase, Philadelphia, PA for twelve years.

Rev. Mike is licensed by the teaching of Intuitional Metaphysics to practice Spiritual Healing and Scientific Prayer. Mike is also a Prayer therapist.

Rev. Mike was elected in 2007 to the status of "Fellow of the American Institute of Stress."

In 2008, Rev. Mike became a practitioner of Coincidental Recognition as he incorporated the CoRe System into his spiritual healing practice.

In 2009, Rev. Mike trademarked a new healing process called Quantum Quatro! Subtle Energy System Support®.

In 2011, Rev. Mike joined the outreach program known as the Health Advantage Group.

In 2012, Rev. Mike became a Certified Professional Coach by The Master Coaching Academy and Joined the Personal Empowerment Group.

Before his Metaphysical, Ministerial and Coaching studies, Rev. Mike worked for Sears Roebuck and Co. while in High School and after graduation, until he joined the U. S. Air Force in 1965. He returned to Sears from Vietnam in 1969 and stayed until 1978. His final Sears assignment was as an efficiency expert in Methods - Operational Research and Development.

He volunteered with Burholme Emergency Medical Services from 1969 and is still a Life Member and Board of Directors Member. He started a private ambulance company in 1975 and worked professionally in the field until 2001 when he devoted his full attention to real estate investing, healing, coaching, and writing.

May All Who Read This Be Blessed
AND SO IT IS!

www.ingramcontent.com/pod-product-compliance
Lightning Source LLC
Chambersburg PA
CBHW072048230526

45468CB00019B/1047